THE HUMAN SIDE OF WEALTH

Legacy Lessons from Father to Daughter

GINA CETNAR

Published by So It Is Written, LLC
Rochester, MI
SoItIsWritten.net

Edited by: So It Is Written – www.SoItIsWritten.net

Formatting: Ya Ya Ya Creative – YaYaYaCreative@gmail.com

ISBN: 979-8-9993606-9-4

PRINTED AND BOUND IN THE UNITED STATES OF AMERICA

TABLE OF CONTENTS

CHAPTER 1
SELLING KNIVES

Many people dread getting older, but there are positives to aging. One advantage is the ability to reflect on five decades of my life lessons and experiences. As I do this, many random events and happenings start making more sense, and I now see the bigger picture. I have constantly questioned whether I was on the right path and whether I had made the right career decisions. This plagued my everyday life as a young adult.

I've always loved science classes, and I've been fascinated by the human body. I majored in biology while attending Michigan State University. I was on the pre-med track. My dream was to attend medical school. As graduation approached, I lost interest in the medical field and was burned out from studying. The thought of four more years in school was daunting. When I graduated, I felt more confused than I did when I entered college. I felt like a ship without a rudder.

During my entire twenties, I found myself going from job to job. I didn't enjoy most of them—much less liked them. I was micromanaged on most jobs. I never felt empowered. I never felt like I had influence in the world. It was a very frustrating time, but looking back, I can appreciate all the valuable lessons I've learned along the way from those unimportant jobs.

When I first graduated from college, I had no direction, no job and no clue what to do next. My mom was looking through *The Detroit Free Press* and circled a job position with a decent hourly pay. I called the number, had an interview and quickly learned it was a sales job selling kitchen knives. I wasn't looking for a "sales" job, peddling kitchen knives to people who already owned knives. This position didn't require a degree, let alone a high school diploma. Because I didn't have any job prospects, I figured I'd try it. This job sparked something within me.

> This job continuously pushed me out of my comfort zone, and I realized that I liked the challenges...

I learned valuable people skills, overcame the fear of making calls and asking for appointments, and developed sales and referral skills. I met new friends and gained valuable skills I didn't even know I lacked. I learned a lot about myself and had some fun along the way. This job continuously pushed me out of my comfort zone, and I realized that I liked the challenges of sales. Who knew? I could never have learned any of these things in any classroom.

I sold knives to people who said they already had knives. I would ask them to take a look at my demonstration. Just let me in the door. I had to face rejections, overcome sales objections and get out of my own way! Many people said, "I already own many knives. I don't need any more knives. I'm good, thanks. I'll listen to your demonstration, but I'm not in the market for buying anything." These knives were top quality, made in the USA. People who bought them loved them so much that I'd get referrals and make additional sales. My friend's mother could only afford one knife. She bought it just to help me out, and later said it's the only knife she uses and named it the "Gina knife." I felt so honored! This was the best education I didn't know I needed!

I started this job in January 1994. My grandfather passed away on January 1, 1994. He was guiding me from the other side, gently nudging me, as I had several dreams of him, at a time when I never felt so frustrated and lost without direction or a plan. This sales job helped me focus enough to avoid letting self-pity and negativity consume me. The entire process served as a valuable foundation for my career as a financial advisor today. After being an independent salesperson for a year, I decided to try something different: the corporate world.

Working in customer service and debt collections at Chrysler for over two years, I dealt with angry, upset and dissatisfied people all day long. My parents' friend worked at Chrysler's headquarters in Auburn Hills. He told me to apply for a summer temporary job in the customer service department. The pay was $14 per hour, a great rate at the time in 1996. He told me that this position could potentially get my foot in the door for something else in the future. After working for three months as a customer service representative, that position ended. Chrysler Financial was hiring customer service representatives in its debt collection department. I applied and got the job. I detested this job and thought I had made a mistake accepting this position.

> I was collecting tools for my "tool bag."

I quickly realized I didn't like the corporate environment and being micromanaged. I was in boot camp, getting paid to learn valuable skills in managing unhinged, emotionally charged people. When people got upset, I learned not to take it personally and to speak in a quieter, slower tone. I learned to ask more questions to get control of the conversation. I also learned the power of silence. Looking back now, it was the correct decision—even though I didn't like it at the time.

I worked many more entry-level jobs. I picked up valuable skills from each and every job along the way. I was collecting tools for my "tool bag." I worked as a telemarketer for a company that promoted motivational speakers' books and cassette tapes. The company was called "Yes! A Positive Network" and was located in Auburn Hills. I quickly learned I was making cold calls—another dead-end job. I found myself frustrated again.

Another brief job was being a salesperson for a dating service in Southfield. I would interview prospects and share all the benefits of joining the dating network, including access to other members' information. This was pre-Internet, before Match.com and other online dating sites. My job required me to get people to pay thousands of dollars in full. I found myself in a high-pressure sales job. It was incredibly stressful because I didn't like being pushy and forceful. My sales closings were extremely low and after three months, the boss asked me to leave. I was devastated! I thought I was a failure. My self-confidence took a big hit. I realize now that I didn't fail; I was only redirected to another path. Reflecting, I'm grateful for these negative lessons that taught me to be humble, resilient and persistent.

My father had been in the insurance and investment business since 1967. He had gone through a nasty business divorce with his partner in the late 1990s. Around that time, I was newly married and working in yet another unfulfilling job. I complained about it to my father after he asked how

I liked my new job. I wondered if there was something inherently wrong with me.

"Why not get your securities license (Series 7) and learn my business?" My father suggested. "This is a great business because you get to help people, and it's very satisfying."

In order to sell or solicit a broad range of securities like stocks, bonds, Exchange Traded Funds (ETFs), and mutual funds, you need a Series 7 license. To register for the exam, you need to be affiliated with a sponsor, which in my case was my dad's broker-dealer. I ordered the self-study book that included quizzes and tests at the end of each chapter. I worked my way through that book, which took six months. Then I took a one-week prep class through Kaplan in Southfield. On a fall day in October 1999, I sat for the six-hour exam and passed. That was my official entry into this business.

From there, I obtained additional licenses, including the Series 66 (IAR = state-level authority), the Series 24, and my life and health insurance license. The Series 66 exam covers state laws and is administered by FINRA, the Financial Industry Regulatory Association. It helps protect investors by regulating U.S. brokers. The Series 24 exam enables one to become an Office Supervisory Jurisdiction (OSJ). To run a branch office, this important designation is required. While I was getting all the necessary licenses, I worked as an assistant to one of the financial advisors at my dad's firm for a few years before becoming a financial advisor and building my own client base years later.

There's no substitute for the experience.

My path is unusual. Most people get their start by working for a large wire house like Merrill Lynch, Fidelity, Primerica, or at a bank or insurance company. These businesses have a budget, staff and resources to train inexperienced people. Most people get their start at these places because of the coaching/mentoring and training. My dad got his start this way by working for Investors Diversified Services (IDS), which is now Ameriprise. Obtaining all the necessary licenses and credentials is the first step to entering the business of personal financial planning. There's no substitute for the experience.

How do you get that experience? Jump in and just do it!

I took a leap of faith by obtaining all these necessary licenses, not knowing at first if I would actually love this career. What kept me motivated and engaged was the opportunity to collaborate with my father and learn from him. He was very passionate and enthusiastic, and he loved what he did every day. He was extraordinarily successful. I had a fervent desire to learn from the best. He also had my best interest at heart and quickly became my best mentor— not only in this career, but in life.

CHAPTER 2

MY FATHER
The Rainmaker, The Connector

Unlike my previous jobs, which were repetitive and monotonous after a brief period, my new work environment was very different. This work environment was much more relaxed.

Not being micromanaged was a huge relief. I didn't have to punch a time clock, which was a big game-changer. Every client's situation was unique, eliminating the monotony I'd experienced in previous jobs. Plus, there was so much to learn. In fact, the education was practically nonstop.

I joined my dad's firm in late 1999—the tail end of the roaring nineties, when everyone was happy making money in the ever-increasing dot.com stock market. This was a small business with a few financial advisors and support staff. Mel, one of the advisors in my dad's office, needed a new assistant. The timing was perfect because I just passed my Series 7 Exam. Much to Mel's delight, I filled the vacant position and became his new assistant.

> Much of what I've learned came from observing and asking questions...

I had the additional "book" knowledge of the industry after six months of studying and passing that exam, but I lacked experience. There was no formal training; I learned from trial and error. It was up to me to be proactive. Asking the right questions and seeking out new tasks and projects were pertinent to my growth and development in this new role.

Every day was an adventure of learning new things—not only in the office, but in the industry as a whole. The Internet was still new, and its emergence prompted companies to adjust their business practices. I was excited to be a part of that evolution. I shadowed Mel and my father during their own client appointments. Much of what I've learned came from observing and asking questions during those appointments, completing all applications to open new investment accounts, and following up with clients and investment companies. I learned a lot from wholesalers who represented annuity and mutual fund companies. Their job was to update us on the latest products, share market updates, and offer sales ideas. I also attended regular CE (continuing education) classes and lunch meetings to keep up on my securities licenses and the ever-changing tax and estate laws.

Not only did I learn about the financial planning and investment industry, but I learned more about who my father is as a person than I did living with him during those first twenty-five years of my life. As a young child, he worked long hours to establish his own business. He took a huge risk branching out on his own. Most of his time and energy went into building his business and nurturing client relationships to ensure future success. My sister and I didn't see him much at home. Many evenings, we were already in bed when he got home. Many mornings, he was already

> My father always said, "People don't care how much you know; they just want to know how much you care."

gone by the time we got ready for school. As a teenager, I was occupied with my own social life. Then, I moved away to Michigan State University for four years.

My father was very passionate, motivated, driven and always full of ideas. He called himself "the rainmaker," stirring up opportunities so others could implement and carry them to fruition. He was outgoing and made friends wherever he went. I observed how he treated his clients— just like old friends. He made strangers feel like family, and he always found common ground with people from all walks of life.

My father always said, "People don't care how much you know; they just want to know how much you care." He always reminded me that establishing rapport builds trust. People will do business with those they know, like *and* trust.

What stood out to me when I shadowed him in client meetings was that he discussed money and finances for only a small part of the meeting. The rest of the time was spent talking about their families, travel, golf, and other common interests outside of money. Most of the time, he knew his clients' mutual friends. He knew more about his clients and their family dynamics by taking the time to ask questions and listen intently. He was a "connector" of people. He often told me, "This is a relationship business. It's not really about the money. It's 80% relationships and 20% technical knowledge, which is also especially important."

As I sat in on his appointments, I had the privilege of hearing him share stories with his clients about his childhood, goals, dreams, hopes, and fears. I never knew until he revealed them to them. In fact, I learned more about my grandparents—his parents—through his storytelling. It was interesting to see him in a new light, as a regular person rather than a parent. It felt like I was meeting him for the first time. One of the more interesting stories he told was about the time he experienced his first significant loss: his beloved grandfather.

He shared a time when he was eleven years old and he lost his maternal grandfather. The night before his grandfather, Domenic, passed away, he had a nightmare that he was trapped in a car with a giant snake wrapped around it. He was remarkably close to his maternal grandfather, as he was the first grandchild and only grandson. His grandfather bought him expensive boots that his parents couldn't afford. He would take him to the store and let him pick out anything he wanted. He bought my dad special things that his parents couldn't provide. My dad was devastated when his grandpa passed away. He was mad at God. It was the first death of someone very dear and close to him. Instead of trying to impress clients with all the technical knowledge and industry jargon, my father would ask them, "How are you doing? What's going on in your family and on your job?" One of his favorite things to ask about was their health. Health is wealth. It doesn't matter how much money you have if you're not able to enjoy it due to health reasons. He would ask how their relationships with their children and grandchildren were. He always asked clients about their personal lives. One question would be, "How do you want to be remembered when you're gone?" This would prompt clients to think about legacy planning.

People want to be remembered in a positive light when they're gone. An example of being remembered in such a way would be setting up college accounts for young grandchildren. He would encourage them to take that trip and create memories with the kids and grandkids. My father would always say that people with money die with their money. Therefore, he reminded his clients that we don't get to take the money with us when we die. You'll never see a U-Haul following a hearse.

Shadowing my father allowed me to see him in a new light. Not only was I able to witness his brilliant way of connecting with clients, but it was also interesting seeing him as a regular person, not as "Dad." It felt like I was meeting him for the first time.

CHAPTER 3

THE MOTHER OF ALL JOBS

I stepped away from my job as an assistant at my dad's firm to be a full-time, stay-at-home mother after having my first son in 2002. I had no definite plans for how long I'd be at home, or if I would even go back into that business. My husband was in the mortgage business and part-owner of a small brokerage firm in Southfield. He was doing well enough to support us on one income, and he was incredibly supportive of my staying at home.

> We delayed much instant gratification, lived below our means and built up our emergency funds.

We were married for four years before we had our first son. This was no surprise, and we had prepared for it. We discussed ahead of time how we would make it work on one income so that I could be home. We delayed much instant gratification, lived below our means and built up our emergency funds. Doing this enabled us to invest generously in our retirement accounts.

In our early years of marriage, we made significant financial decisions based solely on his income, including securing a mortgage for our new house. At the time, he was doing well financially. We could have qualified for a much larger house and mortgage, but resisted that urge. We bought a 1,800-square-foot modest house in a nice Troy neighborhood with good schools. My income wasn't as robust as his, so we put it into savings and my Roth IRA to build our future.

Another reason I stayed home was that it didn't make sense to pay for childcare since I wasn't a high-income earner. I felt a strong instinct to be home with my son. I couldn't fathom having someone else spend a big part of the day bonding with him while I was gone. God had a hand in all this planning. Had I earned a high income, it would have been more of a challenge to step down and give that up. In fact, I always had that strong maternal instinct to be the main caretaker of my children, years before I even had them.

Several weeks before I had my son, I had a vivid dream that I showed up for work and there was no desk or workspace available for me. I was frantically trying to get home because I forgot to feed my baby. All I wanted to do was get back home to him. Not only was this another sign guiding me to stay home, but it validated and supported how I truly felt deep inside.

Our neighborhood elementary school closed due to low enrollment. It was later converted to a daycare center in the late 1980s, long after my sister and I completed elementary school. My mother is old-fashioned and very opinionated. Being a stay-at-home mother, Mom had a strong opinion concerning the women she observed dropping off their infants and toddlers at the daycare center. She made many derogatory comments about how these women were missing the major life milestones with their babies.

> A mother has to make the best decision for her family and personal situation.

"Why even have children if you're not going to raise them?" My mother would often say. She commented on how little time women had left after a full workday to spend with their children. "Spending time with your young children is so important," she said. "The time goes by so quickly and you never get that back." She also told me, "You can always go back to work when they're older and in school." I didn't realize it at the time, but her comments made a deep impression and left an indelible mark on me. It would take another decade or more to realize this when I was about to start my family.

I do realize that there are no right or wrong decisions. A mother has to make the best decision for her family and personal situation. Some mothers don't have the option to stay home due to financial constraints. Some mothers don't want to stay at home and feel they are better parents by working and providing financially for their families.

I thought being a full-time, stay-at-home mother would be a piece of cake. I would get to stay at home and sleep in. I wouldn't have to set an alarm clock. I didn't have to answer the boss. I didn't have pressured deadlines to meet. I didn't have to deal with office politics or drama. I envisioned having all this spare time to organize my house, clean out my closets, and cook new and fancy meals while my baby was blissfully napping. It turned out to be a major character builder and turned my life upside down! It was a rude awakening!

Becoming a mother was the most challenging job I've ever had. There were times I asked, "What did I get myself into?" Then I would feel major guilt because there were childless women who were frustrated because they couldn't get pregnant so easily. Other parents had children with health challenges or special needs. My baby was healthy. So, what was I complaining about?

I finally understood what experienced mothers and fathers told me about parenting being extremely demanding work. Their words were empty and meaningless until I was in that exact situation. It took a few years to get used to being a full-time mother. The most challenging part of being a mother was the lack of sleep in those first six weeks after coming home from the hospital with my firstborn son. After I adjusted and got into a nice routine, I had my second son almost two years later. Those first several years were challenging because I felt isolated from the world. I had a two-year-old and an infant, both in diapers. My two young babies constantly needed my attention and energy. If I wasn't preparing meals, I was cleaning up after them. I barely got to cook a full dinner, and I ate standing up at the counter. I would get through my day and think that I had nothing to show for all the work I did.

This job was not as glamorous as it was perfectly depicted in *Parents* magazine. I had a monthly subscription and read them cover to cover while expecting my first son. It showed smiling mothers and cute babies, all impeccably dressed. Everyone always looked perfectly clean, happy, and well-rested. My life at home didn't reflect any of that!

I mourned my former life of carefreeness and the ability to come and go as I pleased. Being fully responsible for others' lives was a huge adjustment. Having children made me fully appreciate my own parents, especially my mother, and what they sacrificed. They must have had these same uneasy thoughts and feelings that I had when they became parents.

Another epiphany was when my good friend's mother-in-law came over to visit shortly after I had my first son. Her nursing career spanned over three decades and she raised four of her own children. She was an experienced and natural caregiver. She loved watching her own grandchildren. As she held my infant son, she looked over at my coffee table. There were a few parenting books and magazines on the table. I'll never forget the words she said to me.

> I remembered her wise words: "Trust yourself. You're the expert." At that time, I didn't believe her.

"Burn those books. You're the expert," she said. At the time, they were just words. But her words resonated deep within me, and I didn't forget them.

As the years went on, I had to make many major decisions that shaped my children's lives and futures. This was one of the hardest parts of parenting, and it was intimidating. Whenever I faced a major decision, I always recalled that day when my friend's mother-in-law came to visit. I remembered her wise words: "Trust yourself. You're the expert." At that time, I didn't believe her. I remember thinking, *Me? An expert? I just had a baby and don't know what I'm doing.* How could I qualify as an expert? I always thought everyone else was the expert, especially if they had credentials after their name. I didn't have any of that! Her words ignited a spark within me and became more believable as time went on.

I read a book about sleep training and the *Cry It Out (CIO) Method*. The author, a Ph.D., suggested letting your baby cry themselves to sleep. The reasoning was that they would be trained to soothe themselves and be less dependent on their mothers. The book went on to say that after several weeks of being consistent with letting them cry it out, the baby would eventually fall asleep right away. Logically, this made sense; I agreed with this so-called expert.

The first night, I laid my son down in his crib and walked out of the room. He was about six weeks old, and I was anxious to get him on our sleep schedule. He instantly started screaming and crying as expected. My husband and I sat in the family room, waiting for him to tire himself and fall asleep. After a torturous five minutes, I couldn't stick with this author's plan. I could hear my friend's mother-in-law's words in that instant: "Burn those books! You're the expert." I honored my maternal intuition and threw that book into the garbage.

I walked upstairs and rescued my son. I picked him up, held him and rocked him to sleep. This felt right and I was relieved. I did this until he was old enough to fall asleep on his own. I realized that it doesn't matter what some Ph.D. or expert says, or what the latest trends are. I listened to my own heart and did what felt right for me. I have no regrets!

I'm happy to report that I didn't spoil my baby. He grew up quickly and didn't need me to rock him to sleep anymore. He is a well-adjusted adult today and falls asleep without any help from me. What I wouldn't do to go back to those precious times. At the time, it felt like eternity —

like your life was stuck in an unchangeable, permanent situation. What I learned is that when those moments are overwhelming, stand back and look at the big picture. Know that life is always in flux, always changing. Nothing lasts forever. Babies grow up and change, and your life changes along with theirs.

I stayed home with my two boys for seven years. I participated in all their school activities. Life got easier as they got older and more independent. I met some nice preschool moms as I became involved with Troy Co-op Preschool. I finally got a break when my oldest son was in first grade, and my younger son was in preschool. Then, the Great Recession of 2008 happened.

CHAPTER 4

ECONOMIC RELAPSE

In 2008, the economy started to show signs of weakness and instability. My husband's business was negatively impacted and slowed down quite a bit. The news was constantly reporting layoffs across all job sectors. Economic data showed reports of the economy contracting. People were not putting their houses on the market, so they weren't getting mortgages. The mortgage industry slowed down to a trickle.

The U.S. economy was in a precipitous decline as people lost their jobs. Manufacturing slowed to a halt, and major financial institutions such as Bear Stearns, AIG, and Lehman Brothers collapsed. The U.S. markets plunged, and the decline spread to markets overseas, as the entire world was engulfed in the Great Recession of 2008 and 2009.

My husband's mortgage business began to slow in late 2006, just as the housing bubble was peaking. He and his business partners knew the subprime (high-risk) lending market would eventually blow up because of the extremely lax lending criteria set by the Clinton administration in the 1990s. They didn't think their business would be adversely affected because they dealt only with people with good credit. They didn't consider another plan of action because once this blew by, they thought it would eliminate much of their competition. If they could only wait and ride out the storm, they would be better off in the long term. Unfortunately, this plan didn't work out.

> The world economy plunged deeper and deeper into a recession. Homeowners defaulted on home loans.

As the Great Recession worsened, my husband and his partners closed their business. The subprime housing market negatively impacted his mortgage business. We had no income. We lost a significant amount of our nest egg in the stock market in late 2008. It was truly a stressful time, to say the least.

The world economy plunged deeper and deeper into a recession. Homeowners defaulted on home loans. Unemployment rose to 10% in late 2009. Some banks failed and even needed government intervention. The U.S. economy shrank for several consecutive quarters with no end in sight. This eventually impacted all businesses, including commercial and individual borrowers with excellent credit. It was a terrifying time—not only for our household, but for our city, state and country.

The City of Troy discussed closing down our library and community center. The elementary school that my older son attended cut back on certain enrichment classes, such as Spanish and Art. The twelve Troy elementary schools staggered their start and end times so they could lay off six of the bus drivers. There was a lot of uncertainty and fear during this time.

We had extraordinarily little income for well over a year, so we had to cut back on everything drastically. My husband accepted a part-time, temporary accounting job at his good friend's construction company in Detroit. This helped bring in some money, but it wasn't enough to cover all our bills. We ended up liquidating our retirement investments and had to pay the early withdrawal penalty (under age 59½) to free up extra cash.

Our other investment account, which had accumulated and grown over the years, fell sharply in value as markets continued to drop. Day after day, we watched our accounts fall in value. We wondered if there would be anything left! The bottom fell out for us as we lost the security cushion we had worked so hard to build. We had to liquidate all our assets over that year and a half to stay current with our mortgage and other basic living expenses. Despite these circumstances, we still managed to pay our bills on time to protect our credit scores.

> She gave me her credit card to buy groceries. I felt so terrible and sick to my stomach that I had to rely on my parents.

Thankfully, my parents helped us out. One day, my mother came over to watch my boys as I ran errands. She gave me her credit card to buy groceries. I felt so terrible and sick to my stomach that I had to rely on my parents. It felt like I'd hit rock bottom. I was in the checkout line and broke down. I cried as I approached the cashier. I tried to keep it together, but I just couldn't. It was extremely embarrassing. The bagger who was packing my groceries consoled me.

"Are you okay?" The bagger asked. I was so choked up that I couldn't answer her verbally. I didn't want to answer her and spill my heart out in a public place. She gave me a tissue and told me, "Everything will be okay."

Every day, I woke up with a heaviness of depression, fear, worry and gripping anxiety. I watched our savings and checking accounts dwindle down to nothing. My husband and I were stressed every day. He is the type of person who doesn't complain or vocalize his feelings. He kept everything inside.

During this time, my husband was solely working as a temporary account worker. I was still at home with my boys. My older son was finishing first grade, and my younger son was completing his last year at Troy Co-Op Preschool. Mentally, I was preparing to go back to work. I felt the urge to use the securities licenses I earned while working as an assistant at my dad's firm.

I've never felt so helpless and hopeless in my entire life. It didn't make it any easier to see friends and family moving along and getting ahead while we were falling behind. I know better than to compare myself to others, but it was hard not to. I felt like I lost control of everything.

One of the positive things I did for myself was working out. I was in the best physical shape of my life and enjoyed my workouts at Lifetime Fitness. It was my escape from the financial chaos and stress of feeling helpless. This was the only area I felt I could control completely, so I focused intensely on my personal fitness. This helped manage my anxiety and depression. So, I didn't feel the need to take pharmaceutical medications. I always felt uplifted after my workouts. It always puts me in an improved mood to be a better spouse and parent.

> Despite the chaotic uncertainty that plagued my heart, I've learned that there is something we can do to bring peace and joy in the midst of the storm.

Despite the chaotic uncertainty that plagued my heart, I've learned that there is something we can do to bring peace and joy in the midst of the storm. In my case, exercising daily was my refuge. This economic crisis, albeit unfortunate and distressing, was only for a season. In a matter of time, the dark clouds began to lift; soon enough, the sunshine broke through.

CHAPTER 5

ECONOMIC RESURGENCE
Back to Work

Many financial advisors nationwide left the business during these tumultuous times. Some retired earlier if they were in a position to do so. My dad had been trying to find established and successful advisors to join his firm for quite some time. One of the advisors at Dad's firm retired after over 50 years in the business. The other advisor left and started his own company. This left these two offices unoccupied, so my dad encouraged my husband and me to join his firm.

While talking to my father about coming back to work when the boys started school, he encouraged me. He told me his company was a great business to be involved in.

"You get to be your own boss and control your own destiny," he said. "You have an amazing opportunity to learn about this business from me. I won't work forever, and you have this fortunate opportunity to gain experience from me. I have all these decades of experience you can draw upon and learn from me."

He also reminded me of why it was so important that I kept my securities licenses current over the past seven years: it is so hard to get them again. It's much easier to earn continuing education credits than to lose them and have to get them again.

> Being out of the workforce for over seven years made me apprehensive about returning. It felt like I was jumping back on a fast-moving train.

My husband joined my dad's firm in the spring of 2009, after he passed his securities exams and became fully licensed. I waited until the fall of 2009 to go back to work, when my boys would both start the new school year. I decided to pay for full-time kindergarten for my youngest son, and my older son began second grade. So, they would both be in school all day.

Being out of the workforce for over seven years made me apprehensive about returning. It felt like I was jumping back on a fast-moving train. So much had changed in technology. The printers, computers, and software programs had new and improved capabilities. By this time, faxing was almost obsolete; scanning documents was the new way of sending information to another person or business. I had to learn how to use the new printer and get used to a completely different software platform and CRM (customer relations management) database.

Another area of change in our business was the introduction of more stringent security requirements regarding the client's identity. We had to obtain additional information, such as a driver's license to establish and open new accounts. This was the result of the 9/11 terrorist attacks that happened in 2001.

After being out of the workforce for seven years, my wardrobe needed a major overhaul. My tastes and fashion styles changed along with the latest trends. I committed to 5:15 a.m. daily workouts so I could take my boys to school in the mornings, get to the office by 8 a.m., and be home when my boys were finished with their school day. Fitness remained a high priority. I wanted to continue working out, working full-time, and balance family life, too. Thinking about all this made me apprehensive, wondering how I would manage everything.

I felt unprepared, unequipped and downright terrified of starting this new chapter of my life. But the pain of staying where I was had to be far greater than the pain of change and facing the unknown. I was certainly in a reactive situation and had to take that leap of faith. There was a lot of negative self-talk that I had to overcome and manage. These self-deprecating phrases played over and over in my mind. They were subtle, lurking in the background of my mind: *You can't do this. You're not smart enough, experienced enough, outgoing enough. You're a slow learner. What if you don't make it? What will people think if you fail? What if this isn't the right path for you?"* This was a pivotal time in my life where I had to face and deal with my low self-worth and low self-confidence from childhood. My low self-worth/self-confidence stemmed from early childhood when I was picked on

> Self-awareness is the first step to changing. After becoming aware of these thoughts and old mind patterns, I would say affirmations to counter them.

in school for having darker skin. Several kids bullied me in elementary school. Also, my parents told me, "Children should be seen and not heard!" That had a strong impact. It's amazing what children absorb and believe from others. No longer could I deny or ignore it if I wanted to grow and advance professionally and personally.

Self-awareness is the first step to changing. After becoming aware of these thoughts and old mind patterns, I would say affirmations to counter them. I would say, "I'm smart and capable" and "I'm perfect for this business." It didn't feel believable at the time. Still, I would repeat positive affirmations over and over to counter negative self-talk. This wasn't a quick fix. It took me many years to gain self-confidence and build my self-worth.

It is often said that we are our own worst critics; that was the case with me. Starting anything new is thrilling and scary at the same time. I was excited to take on this unique and rare opportunity that would change the course of my life. Part of success is not only recognizing an opportunity, but also seizing it.

After walking my boys to Leonard Elementary on their first day of school, we took many pictures with our new classmates and teachers. I had knots in my stomach as I left them at school and drove to the office for my first day. I had no clients and limited experience. I wondered how I would make this all work as I transitioned from a stay-at-home mother to a working mother. How would I balance giving 100% at work and 100% at home as a spouse and parent? I had all these worrisome thoughts.

My dad had prospects and former clients in the company database. He also had smaller clients who had one investment account opened years ago, but they weren't active or hadn't been in the office for a review in years. I sat at my empty desk in front of the computer. I felt like I didn't know enough. I wasn't ready to take on my own clients. He gave me some sage advice.

"The goal is to get on the phone, make calls and schedule appointments. That's it. The only way to make money and be successful is to sit face to face, kneecap to kneecap, with prospects."

"Don't try to sell anything over the phone. Just get the appointment. Prospecting is the lifeblood of this business. It doesn't matter how many details you know about investments or specific products. If you don't have people to talk to, you can't make it in this business."

"This is a relationship business. You need to know just a little more than the person you're sitting across the desk from. You will learn and gain knowledge as you go along. The best way to get experience is by talking to people."

My father often shared stories of certain colleagues he had worked with earlier in his career. One of his colleagues, Fred, attended every class offered and knew how every insurance and annuity product worked, but he had barely any clients. How can you make a good living if you are always in class learning, but not out there prospecting and selling? He reminded me that you can always get the answers later. Competency is important, but my dad would say it's only 20% of the business. Maintaining good, solid relationships is 80% of this business. I had a challenging time believing him at first. It took years for me to realize he was right.

As the economy turned around in late 2009, my dad had been working with a third-party money manager who had done a tremendous job of saving his clients from major market losses in 2008 and early 2009. This guy was an excellent speaker who gained a lot of credibility amongst all the clientele. He came into town regularly and spoke about his investment methods and the market outlook as we recovered from this recession.

After a few weeks of getting acclimated to my work routine, I wrote a letter to all my prospects. I announced that I'd joined my father's firm, Financial Solutions of Michigan, as a financial advisor. I further stated how excited I was about this new and wonderful opportunity. I explained that I was fully licensed and had prior experience as an administrative assistant. I expressed my openness to taking on new clients. I also let everyone know that my sons attended Leonard Elementary School and that I was actively involved as a parent volunteer on field trips, helping in the classroom with holiday parties and other school activities.

I mailed this letter to all the parents in my son's elementary school directory. I sent a letter to over two hundred people and later followed up with phone calls. Some of the parents I knew personally because their child was in one of my son's classes. Most of the people I didn't know well enough, but I wasn't afraid to try. What did I have to lose? If you don't ask, the answer is always, "No."

I followed up by leaving numerous voicemail messages. A few parents called back; however, most people weren't interested in working with me. They either had an established relationship with another advisor or gave some random reason for not scheduling an appointment with me. I ended up with three people who agreed to attend our money manager's upcoming seminar. Out of those three who attended, I ended up with one client. The rejection rate was extremely high, and I felt defeated.

My enthusiasm faded quickly, and I started to doubt myself. I questioned whether I'd made the right choice and whether this was the right path for me. That inner critic was strong and persistent. The first few years were challenging, even though I'm not a stranger to rejection. Many of my previous jobs involved sales—either direct sales, phone sales, cold calling or telemarketing.

All these past dead-end jobs helped prepare me for future rejection. It toughened me up.

In the meantime, I kept calling prospects and inactive clients in the database. I worked on paperwork, sat in on my dad's appointments, and learned as much as I could. I read and studied all the latest insurance and annuity products and how they worked.

Not only was the current economic landscape still a challenge, but many people were also still frightened by the markets. What if we weren't out of the woods with this recession? What if there was a double dip in the market? Many people were reluctant to invest, especially after seeing their retirement investments lose half their value. By the second quarter of 2009, the markets and the economy began to recover slowly.

There were many challenges for a new advisor entering the world of personal financial planning. For one, several prospects questioned their trust in financial advisors after Bernie Madoff dominated the news headlines in 2009. Bernie Madoff faced major legal consequences for orchestrating the largest Ponzi scheme in history. Madoff was arrested on December 11, 2008, but the legal process unfolded throughout 2009, during the time that I began my career. He was charged with running a decades-long Ponzi scheme that defrauded thousands of investors out of an estimated $65 billion. This was another hurdle I had to overcome. Thankfully, this eventually faded away as other news stories unfolded and took center stage.

> It took five years before we built up our emergency bank accounts and began investing in retirement accounts.

Most people get their start by working for large wire houses like Merrill Lynch or Fidelity. A wire house is a full-service broker-dealer that offers a wide range of financial services, including investment advice, financial planning and retirement planning. These companies have different business structures and vast resources to train new advisors. At my dad's small firm, I had to ask other employees questions and rely on them for help.

Even though my husband and I faced a lot of uncertainty, financial instability, fear, stress, and rejection from prospects and some family members, we felt fortunate for this incredible opportunity. Yes, even some of my family didn't want to do business with me, and they were in that category of prospects. We were able to start earning income and get our financial house back on track. This process was slow at first. It took five years before we built up our emergency bank accounts and began investing in retirement accounts. Most of our investment accounts were closed because they had a zero balance. We started all over again.

> God works in mysterious ways. I now appreciate those challenging times. It pushed me to step way beyond my comfort zone and grow personally and professionally.

If my husband hadn't lost his business and continued on the trajectory toward success in the mortgage business, my path would have been completely different. As I look back on this entire experience, I am grateful that it led me to work with my dad and to get to know him better as a person. I don't think I would have had the opportunity to establish a closer relationship with my dad. My relationship with my dad in the past was nonexistent. This business helped us find common ground so that we can be much more connected. That is priceless!

God works in mysterious ways. I now appreciate those challenging times. It pushed me to step way beyond my comfort zone and grow personally and professionally. This experience taught me a lot about myself and my relationship with money. I discovered that I had low self-worth.

I felt like I didn't deserve the nicer things in life. That was an eye-opener. I have proactively and diligently worked to change this by changing my thoughts and eliminating negative self-talk. This all led to inner work and self-reflection.

Perhaps you have struggled with self-worth issues in your own life. Maybe you don't feel worthy of success and the finer things in life. Many people feel guilty for "having more" than others. I realized that we are all worthy of abundance and prosperity. It all comes down to our mindset and what we tell ourselves. Pay attention to how you talk to yourself. Then you can proactively make changes. We are a product of our thoughts and beliefs. Once we change our thoughts, we change our lives. The outer world will reflect that back to us. This setback taught me how to change my life by changing one thought at a time.

CHAPTER 6

PLANTING, PERSISTENCE AND PATIENCE

Working and learning in this relationship business allowed me to focus on my personal growth and build my self-worth and confidence nonstop. This process took many years. I knew that if I wanted to succeed in this business or any other career, an attitude adjustment was necessary, along with changing how I viewed myself and my capabilities.

I became very deliberate, intentional and self-aware with my internal self-talk while keenly observing my thoughts. Most importantly, I focused on positive affirmations that affirmed that I was more than capable of thriving in this business. I didn't let rejection or disappointment erode my self-confidence. Many times, I'd slipped back into negative thinking mode. When I found myself slipping back into old thoughts like that familiar self-deprecating talk, I immediately caught it. I turned it around by thinking positive thoughts.

This wasn't a linear, upward learning process. There were many emotional ups and downs. There were days my self-confidence wavered and self-doubt crept in. Some days, it felt like I took one hundred steps backward. I questioned myself, wondering if I was doing the right thing or if this was even the right path. Some days, I wanted to

> I focused intently on my daily behaviors and tasks, which were contacting clients and prospects every single day.

quit. Other days, I felt victorious and on top of the world.

I focused intently on my daily behaviors and tasks, which were contacting clients and prospects every single day. Sometimes it was via email or phone. Other times, I mailed handwritten letters. This gave me confidence because I could control my behavior, even though I couldn't control the outcomes. People either called me back or they didn't. As long as I disciplined myself with daily behaviors, that gave me the confidence to keep going, even when there weren't immediate results. When I followed through on my commitments, I became less concerned with the desired outcomes.

I set daily goals, for example, of calling five to ten people. No matter how busy the day got, I worked this into my schedule. Contacting people and staying in touch is paramount to establishing relationships and trust.

My dad often said, "It takes years to build relationships and establish trust, but it only takes one negative interaction to destroy credibility and trust."

My dad always emphasized doing the right thing, even when no one is looking. He always stressed the client's well-being and needs coming first; the rewards would come later. Gaining worthy clients is like planting good seeds and being patient as the fruit grows. He'd say, "Just keep planting those seeds."

Contacting clients and prospects became easier as I got more settled into my role as an advisor. I developed tougher skin and learned not to take rejection personally. Timing can be everything in helping a client be ready and willing to work with me. If they weren't ready or responsive, I scheduled follow-up calls for six months or a year into the future.

Scheduling appointments was a challenging task. If I got them to commit to meeting me at my office, that was only half the battle. Growing my book of business (i.e., network of clients) was rooted in a simple idea: I gave them my undivided attention, delivered exceptional customer service, and had genuine follow-through. I deepened every relationship by asking more questions—not only about their financial goals and risk tolerance, but about their personal and professional lives. I observed their attitude toward money and asked personal questions to get them to open up and share more about themselves and their family dynamics. By taking the extra time, I was able to uncover new opportunities not only to help them, but also their families, friends, and colleagues. I would simply ask them if they knew someone who would like to work with me and receive personalized service and guidance.

Another opportunity to acquire new clients presented itself in 2012, when one of my dad's former colleagues contacted him about buying his book of business. John was 86 years old and decided it was time to retire, but he wanted to make sure his clients would continue to be well taken care of by someone he knew and trusted. My dad's and John's paths crossed many decades ago when John joined IDS, a financial planning firm that is now Ameriprise. My dad was a general manager at that time. He trained John when he began his new career.

John served as a priest for many years, but he left the priesthood to marry a former nun and start his own family. Choosing the financial investment industry was a seamless and perfect transition for him. He was already part of a vast network of priests, nuns, and clergy members. He knew many families from the parishes he served as their priest. He developed deep, meaningful relationships with these parishioners and fellow clergy. They established trust with him already. As my father has reiterated many times, this is a relationship business built on trust. John had that advantage and was poised to be successful in this business for several decades before retiring. Many of his clients became his closest friends.

We helped write a formal letter to John's clientele, explaining his retirement and assuring them they were in good hands with our firm. John also shared his background, including how he met my dad, worked

> ... we discovered the rewarding nature of collaborating with people who value and devote their entire lives to serving others.

with him in his early career, and how their values aligned. At some point, they went their separate ways but always stayed connected. Now, everything had come full circle.

Acquiring this book of business, consisting of priests and nuns, proved to be a meaningful, strategic addition to our firm. As our firm integrated this new book into our practice, we discovered the rewarding nature of collaborating with people who value and devote their entire lives to serving others.

I didn't grow up Catholic. In fact, I had little exposure to priests and nuns throughout my life. They were more like distant, mysterious figures. The media had a powerful way of shaping my views of the clergy due to negative headlines that were emphasized and plastered all over the news. My general perception of priests was shaped negatively by the media's influence. That all changed when I began collaborating with them in my role as a financial advisor.

Honestly, I wasn't sure what to expect. Would they be guarded? Would I understand their world? Would they even want to talk about money? Some people view money as something that's "nonspiritual." To my surprise, they welcomed me with grace and humility. Through our conversations, I began to appreciate the richness of their lives. Many chose simplicity and made sacrifices in service and dedication to others. Several of the priests had a funny and unique sense of humor. One priest appreciated fine wine and enjoyed conversations about current events. Another priest loved good Italian food. Many weren't concerned with wealth but with sustainability and leaving behind a solid legacy for their families, churches, and charities.

I was fortunate to attend my client's sixty years of service in the priesthood. Saint Regis Church in Birmingham held a mass and celebration afterward to commemorate Father Murphy's service. The church was packed that day, with standing room only. Generations of parishioners came to honor him. He was well-liked and respected, and I felt lucky to have collaborated with him for six years before his passing. It was a great honor to get to know him on a personal level.

Over time, I learned to appreciate the humor and dedication of the priests and nuns. Collaborating with them didn't just expand my book of business. It expanded my perspective. I'm profoundly grateful for that.

After several years in the business, my dad encouraged me to pursue my Certified Financial Planner (CFP®) designation.

He earned his when the program was brand-new. He was in the second graduating class to get this credential in 1979. He said it would give me more credibility, and I'd earn more respect within the financial investment industry.

When he first recommended obtaining this credential, I wasn't ready. I was still adjusting to balancing work, family, my son's school activities, and other household obligations. How would I manage to include more? I remember my dad studying for the CFP® when I was in grade school. He would lock himself in his bedroom for hours, reading and studying the material. In the summer months, he would sit at our picnic table on the patio, studying intently.

> I knew this would be demanding, but I also knew that growth never happens in comfort zones.

One of our wholesalers, who represented a mutual fund company, informed me that Oakland University was launching its first cohort CFP® program. This was designed for working students from all walks of life who wanted to obtain this prestigious designation. The classes were held on Wednesday evenings and Saturday mornings. It was in late 2013 when I took that leap of commitment, and it was not a decision I made lightly. I knew I would be stepping into a journey that would stretch me intellectually and personally. I knew this would be demanding, but I also knew that growth never happens in comfort zones. I officially signed up for the Certified Financial Planning program offered through Oakland University in January 2014.

It felt like the right time for me. My sons were in the fifth and seventh grades and were more independent. This was a fifteen-month program. It consisted of six separate classes in the following disciplines: Taxes, Risk Management/ Insurance, Investments, Retirement Plans, Estate Planning and the final capstone class. This involved putting together a comprehensive financial plan based on my personal situation, investments, retirement projections, and goals. The capstone gave us the opportunity to utilize all five disciplines and reinforce everything we learned. After presenting the financial plan to the instructor, there was a month of intense study and review to prepare for the six-hour exam at a Kaplan testing center.

Earning the CFP® designation was one of the most rigorous and rewarding challenges I've ever undertaken. It demanded mastery across several complex financial disciplines, relentless focus, and an unwavering commitment. There were late nights, early mornings, and moments where the finish line felt distant. But I stayed the course—driven by a deep belief in the value of guiding others toward financial clarity and peace of mind. Achieving CFP® status wasn't just a professional milestone. It was a testament to what's possible when my purpose, passion, and perseverance come together. I learned so much about myself, my capabilities, and my determination. When I passed that exam on March 26, 2015, I felt a huge relief wash over me! It felt like releasing a deep breath that I'd been holding for a long time. Now, I had the confidence I needed to further advance in my career and continue pressing forward in the face of rejection, challenges, and disappointments.

Obtaining my CFP® designation, working on that new book of business from my dad's old colleague, and doing my daily behaviors helped build and grow my own book of business. My confidence and self-worth grew, and I felt content with my progress. My dad always emphasized prospecting for new business and asking for referrals. He told me repeatedly, "Getting referrals is the hardest part about this business, but it's the most critical. It's the lifeblood of the business." Now that I had five years of experience under my belt, along with my credentials, I felt more confident asking clients for referrals.

CHAPTER 7

TURNING ANXIETY INTO AUTHORITY

Joining the Troy Chamber of Commerce was one of the wisest investments I made for my professional and personal growth. The chamber staff warmly and enthusiastically welcomed me. Shortly after signing up, an ambassador from the chamber came to my office and provided personalized guidance and insight on how to get the most out of my membership. When I joined, I had no idea what to expect since I'd never been part of any chamber of commerce. The original intent was to get new business and network. Little did I realize that I would be forced to focus on my communication skills before I could comfortably network and obtain new business. You'd think communication would come naturally since I do this all day, every day. This wasn't the case for me.

I signed up for my very first event, a J.A.M. session, which means "Just A Minute." Each member gets a turn to speak about their business and give their "elevator pitch" to a room full of people for one minute. It was awkward and uncomfortable. I soon became reacquainted with my biggest fear, one I had spent my entire life running from: public speaking.

My heart raced when it was my turn. I was unprepared. I fumbled and stumbled over my words. My hands became clammy, and my throat got dry. Even though it was uncomfortable walking into a crowded room full of strangers and speaking in front of a group, I still found it exhilarating. I managed to get through that first event and had a terrific time.

> These networking events forced me to think and formulate my own elevator pitch so I could succinctly convey what I did.

The people were receptive, friendly, and inviting. The atmosphere was positive and energetic. I enjoyed learning about others' professions and meeting new people. This was enough—despite my discomfort—to keep signing up for events and getting more involved. These networking events forced me to think and formulate my own elevator pitch so I could succinctly convey what I did. It sounds so simple, but I overlooked its importance.

Following my assigned ambassador's advice, I quickly joined a Business Development Group (BDG) within the Troy Chamber. This was a small-group setting of 15 to 20 individuals who met twice a month. My group met at Walsh College. We got to know each other on a deeper level by sharing what we do in greater detail. We gave each other referrals whenever the opportunity presented itself.

At each meeting, one person had the opportunity to serve as the main presenter for 10 to 15 minutes. I'll never forget the first time it was my turn. I was well-prepared and had my talking points in front of me, but I couldn't shake that deep-rooted fear. Fear overpowered everything. My voice was unsteady, and I couldn't hide my nervousness. The words didn't flow smoothly.

I realized after that presentation that the fear wasn't going to go away on its own. I had to face it head-on.

A fellow BDG member kindly suggested being his guest at his next Toastmasters meeting. I hadn't heard of Toastmasters, but decided to visit. It was a group dedicated to building public speaking and leadership skills. It sounded terrifying, but I joined after that first meeting. This was time-consuming because I had to write and prepare speeches regularly. I had to learn about the various roles Toastmasters has to run the meetings. But I viewed this as an investment in myself. It gave me a safe place to practice and improve. It gave me "stage time."

Week by week, speech by speech, I chipped away at the fear. There were many times I pulled into the parking lot and sat in my car, not wanting to walk through those doors! The hardest part was showing up and dealing with that negative self-talk again. Sometimes, we get overwhelmed by all the minutiae that we easily forget our "why," our purpose. The fear was painful, but I constantly reminded myself of *why* I was doing this in the first place.

Communication skills are as vital to success in business as oxygen is to life. If I wanted to grow and expand my business, I had to overcome this fear. This fear was holding me back from my potential. I have always admired those who can effortlessly get in front of a group and speak with confidence and clarity. I desired to become just like them. In the past, I'd watched opportunities pass me by. I had ideas in my head, but no one heard them. I realized that staying quiet wasn't just keeping me comfortable; it kept me *small*. It was time to move beyond this self-limiting fear.

As time progressed, I learned not only how to organize my thoughts, project my voice, and become aware of my body language, but also how to *believe* in what I was saying. I learned the power of a pause—that uncomfortable silence that I used to fill with unnecessary filler words. I learned to breathe and get comfortable with the silence.

> Embracing these roles helped me see myself in a new light. I was an authority figure, and I began to speak like one.

Toastmasters was more than a group; it was a safe space to grow, socialize, stumble, and shine. It was a platform to hear and express my ideas. Everyone was supportive and gave vital feedback so I could keep improving. Participating regularly in Toastmasters became an incredible journey that enabled me to build and strengthen my self-confidence. The more time, effort, and energy I put into showing up, the more I gained. The results were encouraging. It also gave me the opportunity to take on leadership roles within the club and attract speaking engagements outside of the chamber and Toastmasters.

Another mental block was seeing myself as a leader and role model. Embracing these roles helped me see myself in a new light. I was an authority figure, and I began to speak like one.

My increasing confidence positively impacted my career. One day, I answered a call from a friend of one of my clients. He was a carpenter and said he had much money to invest and was looking for an advisor. He asked many questions over the phone and talked quickly. I told him I needed to schedule an appointment first, and that he could bring all his statements and tax returns so I could assess his financial situation. He resisted and kept asking questions.

"I need to ask you specific questions and gather information so I can give you the correct advice," I replied. He hesitated before he spoke.

"I need an accountant to straighten out my tax situation. It's been a mess after my nasty divorce."

I referred him to a CPA down the hall from my office. A month later, he called to say, "I'm coming by to pick up my tax returns."

We scheduled a meeting on a late Monday afternoon. I sensed his arrogance from the previous phone conversations, but I figured I'd give him the benefit of the doubt. To my surprise, he brought along a friend to the appointment. He introduced me to his friend and asked if he could sit in on the appointment.

"It's up to you, but I'll be asking personal questions about your financial situation," I said. "As long as you're comfortable discussing this in front of your friend, I don't care."

"He's like a brother from another mother. I don't mind if he knows what I have."

As we walked into my office, I could smell alcohol and cigarettes on his breath and clothing. In fact, he was speaking loudly and acting arrogantly, talking about all this money he had to invest and needed help with where to put it. He started interrogating me with a barrage of questions, just like he did on our prior phone calls. I reiterated that I needed to get an overall idea of where his assets are, how they are titled, what types of accounts they are, his risk tolerance, and his time horizon. He didn't answer my questions; instead, he kept rambling. That's when I realized I did not want to work with this person. I didn't have to accept this person into my practice. It didn't matter how much money he had, if he was even telling the truth. He was loud, obnoxious, and obviously drunk. This was not someone I wanted to take on as a client. As he kept talking, I slammed my hand down on my desk.

"I don't want to work with you. Please leave my office now," I said before I stood up and started walking to the door. The look on his face was priceless, like a deer caught in headlights. He was shocked and looked at his friend, who hadn't uttered a single word.

He blinked and said, "Excuse me?"

I caught him off guard! He sat there for a few seconds as I stood at the door, motioning for him and his friend to leave.

> It was like something snapped into place. I had finally chosen self-respect over potential revenue. Peace over pressure.

"Gee, you have a problem with me because I had one drink?"

I shook my head and said, "Please get out of my office."

He stood up and muttered to his friend, "Fine, fine. I guess she has an issue with someone who likes to have a drink after work."

I remained calm but firm as they walked out the door. I felt a huge surge of confidence so strongly. It was like something snapped into place. I had finally chosen self-respect over potential revenue. Peace over pressure. That moment changed me. I finally had confidence and respect for my own boundaries. Saying no is sometimes the most confident thing you can do. The old me would have let him run all over me. She would have let him control the conversation. But not anymore.

A few days passed and I realized he had his taxes done by the CPA down the hall from my office. I walked into Bob's office and asked him about his experience dealing with this person.

"He was drunk when he dropped off his tax returns and drunk when he picked them up," Bob said. I apologized for referring him, and I explained the situation.

"This isn't the caliber of clients I value and work with," I said.

"It was okay to deal with him this time, but I won't prepare his taxes again."

I shared what transpired when I kicked him out of my office. We ended up having a good laugh at the carpenter's expense.

Looking back to 2016, joining the chamber was the push I didn't know I needed. It led me to reclaim my voice—not just in public speaking—but in *life*. The fear didn't disappear; it just lost its power. And in its place, I discovered mine.

Recently, I've stepped into leadership roles within the Troy Chamber that would never have been possible if I hadn't addressed my communication issues. Currently, I co-chair the Leadership Enrichment Group at the Troy Chamber that meets once a month. It's a terrific opportunity for visibility within the Troy business community, and I get to volunteer some of my time helping to run these meetings.

I've had the privilege of being a guest speaker in an undergraduate finance class at Michigan State University for the past two years. This was another experience that I found enjoyable and rewarding. I'm eagerly looking forward to next year and the opportunities I'll pursue.

CHAPTER 8

OPEN, HONEST CONVERSATIONS
Transition of Ownership

My path has never been clearly laid out. Like most people, my life has taken many twists, turns, and detours. It's been full of surprises and changes that I never would have anticipated or consciously chosen. I never thought I'd end up in this profession, in this space, and now a business owner. If you had asked me fifteen or twenty years ago, I would have rattled off a completely different scenario. In high school and college, I pictured myself as an esteemed, respected medical professional walking the hospital halls. I always thought my path would be in medicine. As a child, I was always fascinated with the human body and how it works. As I got older, my interests shifted to health, specifically fitness and healing.

Whenever I attempt to set specific goals, they rarely materialize exactly as I envision. For most of my life, I lived inside a box—one I put myself in. It was made of rigid expectations, the kind that I absorbed from childhood, from society and from my own perfectionist mindset. I had this picture in my head of what life should look like—who I should be, what I should achieve, and how others should see me.

I had figured out my entire life: the career timeline, the financial goals, my personal benchmarks that, in my mind, defined success. I clung to that plan like a lifeline, certain that control was the key to my happiness. I wanted

> I'm still learning to dismantle the old, limiting beliefs as I adapt to my new role as a business owner and branch office manager.

to control every aspect of my life. I feared the unknown, the vast possibilities that came with taking a risk or breaking the mold. I feared judgment, rejection, criticism, and, strangely enough, success. Success meant responsibility. Visibility. Change. It meant stepping out into the unfamiliar and taking on a new and different role, something I never thought I would do. It meant being a business owner.

I'm still learning to dismantle the old, limiting beliefs as I adapt to my new role as a business owner and branch office manager. Going through this process, I have learned so much about myself. It's not about impressing others. It's about shattering my old beliefs about myself and my capabilities. It's about trusting the process and taking one step, one day, at a time. I can be my own worst enemy; I realized I need to get out of my own way.

When I first started in financial investments, everything felt intimidating, especially the Series 7 exam. I remember all the hard work and effort I put into studying for that exam. When I passed, I was so relieved! My dad encouraged me to take the Series 24 exam shortly after, while I had the momentum. I was young and in that studying mode. At first, I resisted the idea. At twenty-eight, I was just getting started in this new business. I could not picture myself in the position of authority. A Series 24 is required to run and manage a branch office, specifically being an Office of Supervisory Jurisdiction (OSJ). Having a Series 24 means being in a position of authority and having all the responsibility for other advisors in the office. I could not envision myself as a branch office manager, supervising others.

"You're on a roll! You may not need it now, but someday, you might be an office manager. Have it in your back pocket, just in case," my dad told me.

So, I signed up, dug back into the books, and studied for this exam. I passed! Years later, I understood exactly what he meant. Having that license didn't just open doors professionally; it planted the seeds of ownership and leadership. It helped me grow into the role I didn't even know I wanted yet. My dad never pressured me. He simply suggested and encouraged me. That encouragement has made all the difference today.

"Just in case," he said. Turns out, just in case became just in time.

Another area where he prepared me to take on his legacy was having my maiden name included with my married last name displayed on my business cards and email signature. He felt that name recognition was an advantage in this industry. He'd spent decades in the Detroit area building his reputation. He had a solid reputation for honesty and fairness with his clients. Reputation and name recognition are impactful in any business.

My dad told his clients that he'd never fully retire. "If you love what you do, you will never work a day in your life," he always said. He poured everything into his business for many years, including his sweat, pride, and identity. It wasn't just work for him; it was a legacy.

He had open, honest conversations with all his clients. He planned to work for as long as he was capable. But if something happened to him, he reminded his clients that they would be well taken care of by me and our office staff. He told his clients, "That's why I have all these younger people in the office."

At first, those conversations were uncomfortable for me. Over time, they became more necessary. Eventually, they became more natural. He was cognizant of his mortality. He often told his clients, "I'm thankful for my health. But as we get up there in age, anything can happen. I can die or become disabled and sick."

Even though he slowed down and spent more time outside of the office, he stayed engaged as much as possible. Dad didn't love the idea of letting go, but he did love the idea of continuity. This was his baby, his life's

> One day, he abruptly called everyone into a meeting to inform us about my mom's medical diagnosis.

work of building and growing his business. It was hard to concede control after more than fifty years in this business.

For years, my dad talked about eventually selling the business to me. But he would always backpedal and say, "Maybe next year." Then came my mom's diagnosis: Parkinson's disease.

My mom's health had been declining for several years before the official diagnosis. She wasn't herself and she struggled daily with unexplained back and neck pain, weakness in her legs, fainting spells and low energy. Everything changed after that. I watched my dad change, too.

He still came into the office, eager to see his clients and catch up with them. But his mind and heart were somewhere else. He was preoccupied with endless doctors' appointments, managing her medications, and thinking about how much time he had left to spend with the love of his life. One day, he abruptly called everyone into a meeting to inform us about my mom's medical diagnosis. He informed us that he would be spending most of his time with her. It was a complicated, dreadful conversation. He put it off for as long as possible, but he couldn't delay it any longer because it was obvious to our office staff. The emotional weight he endured was palpable and visible to all of us.

There were messy logistics and numerous details to be considered. There were back-and-forth discussions with our home office's transition team and a lot of emotional knots to untangle. I know it was difficult for my dad to let go, but the sense of urgency helped move the process forward. Signing all the documents made the transition official and public. Our home office helped write official letters—one from me and one from my dad—addressing each client about the sale and transition of the business. The letter stated that the level of service would remain consistent, as it always had. This was sent out immediately after the contract was signed. The initial process took about six weeks.

> It wasn't just the sale of a business. It was a transition of a lifelong legacy.

Going through the transition was eye-opening for me. It wasn't just the sale of a business. It was a transition of a lifelong legacy. This wasn't just about revenue and profitability. It was a transition of my dad's values, service, and trust. These weren't just clients; they were relationships built over decades. My father wasn't just selling me a company; he was entrusting me with his life's work.

Shortly after we sent out our letters, my dad and I received an outpouring of encouragement and support from our clients. A few clients were concerned about continuity and the future. However, it was a positive response overall.

I'm grateful that I'm not alone on this journey. My husband has been more than a supportive spouse. He's been my teammate, my sounding board, and my rock. Dan has been actively involved in the business since 2009. Where I handle day-to-day supervisory and compliance tasks, he's taken on the unglamorous work of sorting through all the lingering loose ends. He has the patience to sift through the bookkeeping details and persistence to follow through until things eventually get sorted out. The transition hasn't been easy —there are still knots to untangle —but knowing I'm not alone makes all the difference.

Many of our entrepreneurial clients are experts in their industries and are focused on the daily operations. Most of them have no idea about their exit plan, if they even have one. They're so busy growing and managing their businesses, they don't take the time to think about this. My job as an advisor is to ask them those questions. Who will take over when you're not here to run the business? How long do you want to keep working? Do you have a succession plan in place? If not, why? Having these important discussions is the first step. The next step is to collaborate with a trusted attorney who can draft a buy-sell agreement and manage all the details.

Throughout this entire experience—from my first day at my father's firm to buying his business and everything in between—I've always been supported and encouraged.

The right people always show up at the right time. There have been moments in my life that I've felt alone, unsure, afraid, and on my own. One of those moments was when I worried about not being ready to fill my dad's shoes. God always works in mysterious ways. It's never the grand gestures or lightning bolts from the sky. Sometimes, it's the right person with the exact words, showing up at the perfect time. From our annuity wholesaler, who encouraged me to join the Troy Chamber of Commerce, to another mutual fund wholesaler who informed me of the opportunity for CFP® Certification, these people showed up at the right time.

Looking back, there's a pattern that's too perfect to be a coincidence. When I learned to trust the process and let go of the illusion of control, that's when the right people crossed my path and walked into my life. Maybe they've always been there by my side, supporting me and having my best interests at heart, like my dad and husband.

CHAPTER 9

GENERATIONAL WEALTH

> Many people think they need to be wealthy to work with a financial advisor. The truth is that it couldn't be further from reality.

What sets our firm apart is our approach to going beyond traditional investment management. We don't just look at portfolios; we look at the whole financial picture. By integrating tax planning into our strategies, we help clients keep more of what they earn and help build generational wealth. Our holistic approach means we consider every aspect of your financial life—investments, taxes, retirement, estate planning, risk management, life insurance, and long-term care insurance—so that all the pieces work together seamlessly toward your goals. It's not one-size-fits-all advice. We build personalized strategies that adapt as life changes, ensuring our clients feel confident, prepared, and supported every step of the way.

Many people think they need to be wealthy to work with a financial advisor. The truth is that it couldn't be further from reality. Being a financial advisor isn't solely about managing investments; it's about supporting people through every season of life, such as buying their first home, getting married, retiring, experiencing a job loss, or going through a divorce. Money touches every aspect of our lives, and having someone to turn to during those moments brings clarity and peace of mind. You don't need to have millions to deserve that kind of support.

Working with my dad over the years, I learned that no matter how much a person has accumulated over their lifetime, their main fears are outliving their money or running out of money in old age. Clients who have amassed a few million dollars have the same concerns as those with several hundred thousand dollars. Everyone shares this same fear. No matter what the value of someone's portfolio is, most people die and leave behind money. I've witnessed this over the last twenty-five years of being involved in this business. My dad told his clients that most people do not outlive their money, especially since he'd been in the business for over fifty years. He witnessed the same scenarios throughout his career.

Most people think about money in terms of their own lifetime: how to earn it, spend it, save it and invest it for the years they'll need it in their retirement. *True* financial wisdom looks far beyond your own time horizon. Legacy planning considers the years after you're gone, the people you will impact the most, and the influences you'll have long after you're gone. Legacy planning isn't simply about leaving your unspent money behind; it's about creating structure and a purpose for the assets, the values you impart, and the knowledge you pass on to the next generations.

> I've had the privilege of working with many families that involved two and three generations. Without a plan, wealth can evaporate quickly.

I've had the privilege of working with many families that involved two and three generations. Without a plan, wealth can evaporate quickly. I've witnessed that, too. One of our married couples made several million dollars and had no children. However, they had six adult nieces and nephews named as beneficiaries. I assisted with distributing those assets when they both passed away. Each lucky beneficiary received over $300,000. Three beneficiaries kept their money with our firm. The rest took a lump sum or worked with another advisor. The three who saved the money at our firm spent it quickly within two years.

Studies show that 70% of wealthy families lose their wealth by the second generation and 90% by the third. Why is that? Money alone isn't enough. Without a shared vision, financial literacy, candid discussions, and intentional planning, even the most significant inheritance can be squandered through legal complications, poor emotional decisions, or simply a lack of preparation.

Legacy planning ensures financial stability for your loved ones, clarity in carrying out your wishes, and tax efficiency to preserve more wealth. It also involves protecting assets from creditors, poor management, disputes, and maintaining the continuity of family values, traditions, and causes. The greatest inheritances often aren't tangible assets; it's the mindset and habits that sustain and grow them.

Legacy planning is also about emotional and moral inheritance. It's about sharing life lessons, so future generations know where they came from and what they stand for. You don't have to be a millionaire to think about legacy planning. Whether it's a modest sum or a vast fortune, the principle is the same: Be clear, intentional, and generous with your vision and values.

These are some of the discussions we initiate and encourage with clients we've worked with for many years. This goes back to the relationships we've established and to learning about our clients and their family dynamics. That's why we ask many questions: it helps clients open up and share a little bit about their families and final wishes. Then, we can broach the subject of what clients want to happen after they pass on and who they want to get the money after they're gone.

Let's discuss some tips and keys to building and protecting your legacy. First, define your legacy vision. Before signing any legal document, you must be clear on your intentions and ask yourself these questions:

- What do I want my loved ones to inherit? Not just financially, but emotionally and morally?

- Which values do I want to see passed down?

- Are there any special causes or charities to support?

- Should my wealth be distributed all at once after death, or in stages with specific conditions?

- Are the children spendthrifts?

- Are they mature enough to manage a large lump sum of money?

I've collaborated with clients who don't have any children, but they're close to their nieces and nephews. Depending on their age and life stage, they may fund a college savings account, such as a 529 plan. Some will set aside funds for their futures, such as purchasing a house or paying for a wedding.

Grandparents have incentivized their young adult grandchildren to open a retirement account. Whatever amount the grandchild invests for that year, they will match it. The goal is to teach the next generation the importance of investing, discipline, and long-term thinking.

Twenty-five years ago, an older married couple opened seven accounts and purchased a growth security, worth a few thousand dollars for each grandchild. The grandchildren were babies and young children at the time. Both grandparents passed away, and now I'm working with these adult grandchildren. They are so grateful that grandpa and grandma set this money aside for their future. Twenty-five years later, their funds have more than quadrupled in value. Some of them are investing their own money into this account. One grandchild used it to purchase their first house. It's rewarding to witness what these young people are doing with this money. Their grandparents' legacy carries on.

> It's rewarding to witness what these young people are doing with this money. Their grandparents' legacy carries on.

We have many clients who refer their children to our practice who are in their twenties and thirties. Many of the clients have regretted not starting earlier themselves. They are now encouraging their kids to start investing while they have time on their side.

Some financial advisors work only with clients who meet a certain asset threshold. For example, they work with clients who have a net worth of one million dollars or more. My dad never set minimum amounts because of the importance of working with multigenerational families. Today, the twenty-year-old may not have many assets. Still, someday they may inherit a generous sum or receive a large windfall. They will get a job or start a business. We like to guide and educate our younger clients on the importance of investing and the benefits of consistent monthly investing.

I had the pleasure of working with an older couple in their early nineties. They had built an impressive portfolio over the years while raising their five children. They were disciplined about saving for their future while instilling moral values and a strong work ethic in their children. Once they both passed, I helped facilitate the distribution of those assets to their five adult children. They were incredibly grateful to their mom and dad not only for being disciplined savers but also for the memories they shared with their families.

My dad and I attended their parents' celebration of life. We met many of the extended family members at the luncheon. Once the assets were distributed, the family used them to reconnect with their roots. They planned a "trip of a lifetime" to Scotland! All five children, their spouses, and their adult children and grandchildren—about thirty-five of them—enjoyed their time together, exploring their family roots. Their inheritance wasn't about money.

It was a bridge linking their past to the present, creating lifelong memories that spanned several generations. These types of scenarios that I get to witness in my daily work make this job so rewarding. It's a privilege to be a small part of someone's life and help guide them and navigate through the legal complexities of asset distribution.

Another vital key to legacy planning is having the proper legal documentation to carry out your wishes. This is something we discuss with all our clients, especially pre-retirees and those nearing retirement in the next five years or less. We partner with several trusted estate planning attorneys. It's essential to consult an expert—not just a generic online template—to avoid costly mistakes. Tax and estate laws constantly change. Having a trusted and competent professional makes all the difference.

I helped my dad with his clients, who had a sizeable investment portfolio and three children. They were diligent about saving, investing, and having adequate life insurance. They did everything right. Then, they retired. My dad brought up the sensitive and delicate topic of what they would like to happen when they both pass away. It became an emotional conversation when the wife told him that their adult son suffered from alcoholism. They were both emotional as they shared some of the challenges they faced in trying to get him sober. It was a difficult but necessary conversation to have because they were worried he might make poor decisions.

They didn't want to disinherit their son, but they didn't want to put the other children in a difficult position either. A trust was necessary to spell out specific instructions, especially for the struggling son. However, they weren't sure who to name as the trustee. Would their son resent the other two siblings if he came to them asking for additional money? It was a conundrum until my dad suggested a neutral third-party administrator to ensure the trust's assets are distributed fairly. It also removes responsibility and takes the pressure off the other two children. I've witnessed families break apart over money before. Emotions run high, and people can change for the worse when money is involved. Having a well-thought-out plan in place helps when feelings are intense.

> Life insurance is often an essential and powerful tool used for legacy planning. It serves as both a safety net and a strategic wealth-transfer tool.

Life insurance is often an essential and powerful tool used for legacy planning. It serves as both a safety net and a strategic wealth-transfer tool. One of the main reasons we utilize life insurance is that it provides immediate liquidity. When someone passes on, life insurance provides instant cash to heirs. It's income tax-free, making it one of the most tax-efficient ways to pass wealth to the next generation.

My dad always brought up the subject of life insurance, whether it was a young family starting or a business owner with partners. He would ask difficult, pertinent questions, such as, "What happens if you're not around to provide for your family?" or "How would your business partner continue the daily operations without you there?" These questions prompt people to think about worst-case scenarios, which they typically avoid. Our job, as financial advisors, is to encourage people to expect the best, but plan for the worst, just in case.

Many years ago, my dad sold a sizable life insurance policy to a young married man with three young daughters. He was the sole income earner and worked as an electrician in Detroit. My dad encouraged him to purchase as much group life insurance at his union job in addition to selling him an individual policy. One day, he was at work and suffered a tragic accident, and unexpectedly passed away. His wife was devastated! My dad delivered the news to her that she would be financially stable due to the amount of the insurance proceeds. She wouldn't have to sell her house or make any drastic decisions. He helped invest the proceeds and gave her financial guidance as she raised her three children. She was able to remain in her house, ensure her daughters could attend college, and eventually remarry. He said it was very satisfying that, in the face of tragedy, he was able to ensure her financial security when her life was turned upside down.

Insurance can function as an equalizer. Some families face challenges when assets can't be divided equally. For example, if one child inherits the family business, life insurance can provide other heirs with a comparable inheritance, helping maintain family harmony.

Whenever my dad had discussions with business owners, he always mentioned life insurance. That's when he explained that it was a tool that creates stability when uncertainty strikes. It ensures that a spouse doesn't have to sell the business too quickly, that children have a choice to carry the torch, and that employees aren't left wondering if they'll have a job. Collaborating with my dad, I learned that life insurance isn't about planning for death. It's about planning for life, so that when the unexpected happens, the people and businesses we care about most can continue to thrive.

There is a local business owned by two brothers, who became our clients thirteen years ago. The first question my dad asked them was if they had life insurance. Years earlier, they had each purchased term life insurance, but as time passed, their policies expired. The original insurance agent who sold the policies never reached out to let them know. Busy with the day-to-day demands of running a successful business, they weren't aware they lacked coverage.

Asking that question was critical because we promptly began the insurance application process. One brother secured it reasonably quickly. The other brother wanted to lose weight first so he could secure a better rate. This took longer than planned, but he finally got a policy. Not long after that, life threw him a curveball. He was diagnosed with cancer. The treatments were grueling, but he eventually went into remission. One reality hit hard: if he had waited until after his diagnosis to apply, he would never have qualified for coverage again. Another valuable lesson I've learned from my dad is that you get life insurance while you can. Some people are uninsurable the day they're born. Most people become uninsurable at some point in their lives. We don't know when that time will happen, so the best time to secure life insurance is while you're healthy. Life can change drastically in a fleeting moment. As long as you pay the premiums, you're covered, no matter what happens to your health.

> Legacy planning isn't a one-time event. It's an ongoing act of love, stewardship, and vision.

Legacy planning isn't a one-time event. It's an ongoing act of love, stewardship, and vision. When done well, it not only transfers wealth but also strengthens family unity, preserves values, and prepares the next generation for greater success. By taking these steps now, you're ensuring that your story, your hard work, and your values continue long after you're gone.

No matter where you are on this life journey, you can ask your friends or co-workers whether they work with an advisor and what their experience has been like. That would be the first step if you haven't started any planning. Many clients come to me at various stages of their financial and professional lives. I meet people where they are in life. Many feel like they're behind and wish they had taken the initiative to work with a professional a long time ago. I have them focus on what we can do today and moving forward, since they can't go back to the past.

CHAPTER 10

SACRIFICES BEHIND THOSE HOURS
A Legacy of Love and Lessons

Over these last twenty-five years, I've been fortunate to not only work alongside my father but also to learn from him in ways that go far beyond this business. This opportunity would never have presented itself had my husband and I not gone through the horrendous trials of the 2008 recession. At the time, it felt like everything was crumbling all at once: losing a significant amount of money in the stock market, followed by the permanent closure of my husband's mortgage company. It was humbling and frightening to stand in the middle of uncertainty with no clear path forward as this all unfolded. But those challenges became the foundation and impetus of change. Stripped of comfort and security, we had to adapt, rethink our priorities, and take on new challenges. This setback gave me the courage to pursue this opportunity to join my dad's firm.

At first, I saw this opportunity as a way to contribute financially to the household, pay bills, save for retirement, and achieve our financial goals. But as the days turned into years, I realized I was gaining something far more valuable than a paycheck. I was learning about *him*—not just as a professional—but as a person. Sitting beside him, listening to how he spoke with clients, and hearing his stories gave me insight into the experiences that shaped him. I began to see the values he lived by, not just the advice he gave.

In many ways, working with him gave me the chance to reconnect and make up for lost time. Growing up, I often saw him through the lens of long work hours and commitments that kept him busy. Now, sharing this

> From him, I've learned that true success is rooted in solid relationships.

space with him as an adult, I understood the sacrifices behind those hours and appreciated not only what he provided but who he truly was beneath the responsibilities.

Watching how he interacted with his clients, listening to the stories he shared, and observing the consistency of his actions has been more than valuable for me. From his stories, I picked up wisdom that doesn't come from a classroom or textbooks.

From him, I've learned that true success is rooted in solid relationships. He had an uncanny ability to make people feel comfortable, valued, and heard. He never rushed a conversation, and he always took plenty of time to understand what really mattered to them. He listened thoroughly and made people feel their concerns mattered. Relationships are the true currency, and that respect is built one conversation at a time. He's shared many times that was the most important and satisfying part of his career. A takeaway from his career is that he's made many great friends with his clients and built a strong social network as a result.

Another unexpected benefit of interacting with my father daily was learning about his parents—my grandparents. He shared advice he received from his mother and father as a child growing up in the 1940s and 1950s. My grandmother instilled in my father honesty and a strong work ethic. Through his reflections, I started to see my grandparents in a different light. They weren't just the grandparents I remembered from childhood. They became real people with dreams, challenges, and sacrifices, helping shape the man my dad became. Hearing about my grandfather working hard to provide for his family, and what they valued, gave me a deeper understanding of where our family came from.

This felt like a window into history opening up, but in a personal way. I could connect the dots between the lessons my dad carries, the way he lives, and the legacy his parents left him. It made me appreciate my grandparents—not just as a family—but as individuals whose influence continues to ripple through the generations.

My dad isn't active in the business anymore, but that doesn't mean he's gone. He built the foundation of what we do today. While he's enjoying a well-deserved retirement, he's always willing to share his perspectives and give his two cents, as he likes to call it. It's reassuring to know that even though I've taken over, having him as a guide and mentor is a gift. His wisdom comes in smaller doses now, but it still anchors me, reminding me again that this is not only a business, but his legacy.

> It has become a bridge to him, to the roots of our family, and to the realization that the values we live by are often carried quietly, but powerfully across time.

It's hard to believe it's been fifteen months since I took over the business. At first, I felt overwhelmed by the new responsibilities and focused on day-to-day operations. Now that I've settled into my new role, I'm thinking about my own future and what an eventual exit might look like. My two sons, ages 21 and 23, show no interest in the financial planning field, and that's okay. They are "car guys," and I want them to pursue their passions. My older son, Joey, graduated from Kettering University and works as an engineer for Stellantis. My younger son is a senior at Kettering University, majoring in mechanical engineering. Even though their interests aren't in my business, I keep an open mind that someday they could change their minds, just like I did. I don't have all the answers yet, but I know that just as my dad handed the business to me with trust and confidence, I want to do the same when it's time to pass it on.

Working with my father has been one of the greatest privileges of my career. It's become more than a career experience. It has become a bridge to him, to the roots of our family, and to the realization that the values we live by are often carried quietly, but powerfully across time. His lessons continue to shape how I approach not only my work, but how I carry myself every day.

ABOUT THE AUTHOR

While many financial planners focus on dollars and cents, she's focused on legacy and long-term impact. For Gina Cetnar, CERTIFIED FINANCIAL PLANNER® and advisor, her work is more centered around mindset, not just money. Unlike many financial professionals, Gina holds the Financial Industry Regulatory Authority (FINRA) Series 7, 24, and 66 securities registrations through LPL Financial. Additionally, she holds Life, Accident and Health, Variable Annuity, and Long-Term Care Insurance Licensing in multiple states. Committed to helping clients focus on something bigger and grander than just money, Gina educates and empowers them to think about how they want to be remembered long after they're gone.

Whereas some financial leaders get their start at large wire houses such as Fidelity, Morgan Stanley, and Merrill Lynch, Gina's humble beginnings in the industry were orchestrated by one man: *her father*. For more than 25 years, Gina was fortunate to glean from her father in the business as an independent broker-dealer. While her story blends personal and professional struggles and achievements, she is intentional about training clients to think and execute a plan to leave behind not only their tangible assets but also their intangible assets—their values, wishes, and morals. In honor of her father, a mentor, guiding light, and an encouraging source of success in business, Gina dedicated her debut book to him—and left her published success story as a legacy for her children's children.

In her book, *The Human Side of Wealth: Legacy Lessons from Father to Daughter*, Gina highlights her struggles, triumphs, and victories as she seeks her place in the financial advising world. Spotlighting success stories from collaborating with clients across the nation, she offers keys and tips for everyday families and business owners to truly be at peace, knowing that everything will be taken care of when they leave this earth. As a member of The Financial and Estate Planning Council of Metropolitan Detroit, Gina earned her certificate in Personal Financial Planning from Oakland University and obtained CERTIFIED FINANCIAL PLANNER® Practitioner Certification in 2015.

As the CEO of Financial Solutions of Michigan, Gina believes that the strength and longevity of client relationships, coupled with the quality of company teams, best measure success. Always striving to provide the highest level of service to her clients, she seeks to pave the way for future financial leaders and leave a lasting legacy for her family. For more information, email gina.cetnar@lpl.com.